DISASTER!

FIRES

By Dennis Brindell Fradin

Consultant:
Captain Thomas Linkowski
Fire Prevention Bureau
Evanston, Illinois

 CHILDRENS PRESS, CHICAGO

Early firefighting equipment was heavy and awkward, and some pieces required as many as twenty strong men to pull them to the location of a fire.

For my son, Michael Louis Fradin

Library of Congress Cataloging in Publication Data

Fradin, Dennis B.
　　Fires.

　　(Disaster!)
　　Includes index.
　　Summary: Briefly discusses the origin, uses,
starting, and hazards of fire; some famous blazes;
and protection from fire, including the use of home
fire drills and smoke detectors.
　　1. Fires—Juvenile literature. [1. Fires] I. Title.
II.　Series: Fradin, Dennis B. Disaster!
TH9448.F7　1982　　　363.3'7　　　82-9404
ISBN 0-516-00855-2　　　AACR2

TABLE OF CONTENTS

On November 24, 1980, after a long, dry autumn, fire broke out in the San Bernardino Mountains (above) and swept down into the city of San Bernardino. Flames spread quickly because of high winds and because many homes in the area, including the one shown below, had wooden shake-shingle roofs that burn very easily.

1/THE CALIFORNIA PANORAMA FIRE - 1980

During the autumn, Southern California is ripe for fire. Because the region gets little rain between April and November, by autumn the trees and houses are very dry. Autumn is also the time of fierce northeast winds. Called the "Santa Anas," the winds blast through canyons and mountain passes at up to a hundred miles per hour. Many times these winds have picked up a spark from a downed power line or a small campfire and turned it into a huge blaze.

In the fall of 1980, the combination of dry weather and strong Santa Ana winds created very dangerous fire conditions. By November 16, five major fires had broken out in Southern California. Hundreds of people in Los Angeles, Riverside, San Diego, Orange, and San Bernardino counties fled their homes. These blazes killed one person and scorched nearly one hundred square miles of land, but they were just the prelude to a much worse disaster.

On Monday, November 24, Santa Ana winds gusted at ninety miles per hour in San Bernardino, California. At 10:50 A.M., fire broke out at Panorama Point in the San Bernardino Mountains. Fanned by the winds, the fire soon burned along a two-mile-wide front. It headed straight into the city of San Bernardino.

High winds weren't the only reason that the flames spread quickly. Many San Bernardino houses had "shake shingles" on their roofs. These wooden shingles are pretty, but they burn easily. Flying sparks ignited the shingles. The wind tore the flaming shingles loose and hurled them through the air. Many landed on other rooftops, setting more houses ablaze.

California has a plan by which cities help each other during large fires. Within an hour, equipment and fire fighters began to arrive from out of town. Eventually, help came from San Diego, San Francisco, and dozens of smaller cities. Fire fighters from the United States Forest Service and the California Department of Forestry also fought the blaze.

The twelve hundred fire fighters could do little to stop the "Panorama Fire" on that first day. The heat was so intense that some wooden structures burst into flames without being touched by fire. The wind blew the fire fighters' water streams away from the flames. The Santa Anas weren't the only winds spreading the fire. As huge columns of hot air rose within this massive fire, cooler air rushed in to fill the vacuum. This movement of air created strong wind currents. A fire that creates its own winds in this manner is known as a *fire storm.*

As the streets of San Bernardino filled with smoke, people fled their homes. "It got pitch dark, and smoke started coming into our house," remembered John Cataldo. "I told my daughters Joanne and Kathleen that it was time to run out—there was no time to grab anything."

"There were ashes and sparks flying around as we went to the car," recalled John's daughter Kathleen Cataldo. "We were gagging and coughing. It was so dark the street lights had gone on."

"While we were driving away, wooden shingles were bouncing all over the streets and sidewalks," continued John Cataldo. "When those flaming shingles hit the car, I thought it would blow up. But we made it through a big traffic jam and finally got out of there."

Some persons, ignoring the danger, stayed and tried to save their homes. One group of young people used hoses to save

Top: A row of homes on North Park Boulevard burned out of control.
Above: As smoke filled the streets, San Bernardino City fire fighters worked to halt the spread of the flames.
Left: The flying debris shown here was caused by winds in excess of ninety miles per hour.

half a dozen homes. When sparks ignited their clothes, they sprayed each other. Most efforts to save houses failed, however. People fled when the flames got too close or the smoke choked them.

Of the four deaths caused by the Panorama Fire, three occurred because people didn't leave their homes in time. The charred bodies of an elderly couple, Edith and Earl Welty, were found Tuesday morning near their home. Another man died, either of a heart attack or from breathing too much smoke, after trying to fight flames back from his house. The fourth fatality was a woman who suffered a heart attack shortly after leaving her home on that fiery Monday.

Although Monday was the Panorama Fire's most destructive day, the flames continued for six days more. Experts knew that the best way to fight the blaze would be to drop chemicals on it from the air. The planes were ready. But hour after hour, day after day, the wind made it impossible for the planes to take off.

Fire fighters continued to battle the Panorama Fire for six days.

When the winds died down on Friday, planes like this one were able to drop thousands of gallons of chemicals on the Panorama Fire. By Sunday, the seventh day of the fire, its flames were nearly out.

Meanwhile, more than 2,500 professional and volunteer fire fighters continued to battle the Panorama Fire on the ground. Water wasn't their only weapon. Using bulldozers, tractors, shovels, and axes, they constructed *firebreaks.* A firebreak is a strip of ground cleared of trees, grass, and other materials that burn easily. When a fire reaches a firebreak, it is deprived of fuel and subsides in that location. The firebreaks saved entire neighborhoods from the flames. *Backfires* also were used.

A backfire is a fire started on purpose to stop an advancing fire by creating a burned area in its path. When the flames of the main fire reached the burned-out areas, the main fire subsided because of lack of fuel.

By Friday—the day after Thanksgiving—the wind was calm enough for the airplanes to fly into action. Large planes from the California, Wyoming, and Texas Air National Guards blitzed the fire with thousands of gallons of chemicals. The planes also helped put out some of the seven other major fires that raged through Southern California that week.

By Sunday—the seventh day of the Panorama Fire—its flames were nearly out. Judging by the look of San Bernardino, it was amazing that only four persons had died. Two hundred and eighty-four homes were totally destroyed. Forty-nine others were damaged. One neighborhood where

"Chimney Row"

*San Bernardino City Fire Chief
Gerald Newcombe*

only foundation slabs and chimneys remained was nicknamed
"Chimney Row" by the people who had lived there.

The Panorama Fire was also very damaging to the natural
environment. Many animals died in the flames, and many
others left the area because their homes were burned.
Thousands of acres of grass, shrubbery, and trees were
destroyed, too. The loss of so much plant life was a big cause
for worry. Plants help soak up winter rains and thus prevent
floods. New trees, grass, and shrubbery were planted. Until
they grow, however, flooding may be a big problem in the San
Bernardino area.

How did this terrible fire start? "It was set on purpose,"
said San Bernardino City Fire Chief Gerald Newcombe, one
year later. Starting a fire on purpose is a crime called *arson.*
"The arsonist hasn't been caught, but we're still working on
leads to find out who did it."

2/SURVIVORS - PANORAMA FIRE, 1980

What is it like to be in a fire? Those who have lived through one can best answer that question. Here are the stories of just a few of the survivors of the Panorama Fire of 1980.

John, William, and Eric Wiechert

"I knew there was a fire in the mountains because I was listening to the forestry channel on my scanner radio," John Wiechert recalled a year after the fire. The Wiechert house was just a block and a half from the foothills of the San Bernardino Mountains. A forty-seven-year-old computer repairman, Wiechert was home that Monday morning. It was the first day of his vacation. John's wife, Ruth, was at the school where she worked as a classroom aide. The Wiecherts' teenage sons, William and Eric, were attending classes at their high school.

The Wiechert family of San Bernardino

"At about twelve-thirty I fixed myself a little lunch," remembered John Wiechert. "I looked out and saw a red glow at the top edge of the foothills, maybe half a mile away. The fire had jumped across the highway and was heading our way."

Wiechert was attempting to gather some possessions when the electricity in his home went off. "It was like night—pitch dark from the smoke," he explained. "I went outside and saw that sparks were falling like rain over our house."

Instead of fleeing in his car, John Wiechert tried to save the house, which had a shake-shingle roof. "I climbed up onto the roof with the hose and started wetting it down. Whenever a spark hit the roof, I put it out. The wind was so fierce that one time I was blown down from the roof and had to climb back up."

While Mr. Wiechert was on his roof, William and Eric came home from school. Seventeen-year-old William climbed up to the roof and helped his father hose it down. Fifteen-year-old Eric climbed atop the roof of the house across the alley and tried to put out the flames there.

Eventually, however, houses all around them were blazing. "The wind was blowing so hard the fire just kept going and going—nothing could stop it," remembered William Wiechert. "From the roof I could see smoke and orange flames flying everywhere."

"Sparks and balls of flame were flying through the air," John Wiechert continued. "Then a nearby house exploded, and big clumps of debris came flying overhead. By then the police were yelling at us to leave, and we did."

The police told the Wiecherts to go to the Orange Show Fairgrounds, where the Red Cross had set up an emergency shelter. Eric went in one car with his dad, and William drove

Nothing was left of the Wiecherts' house but a brick wall and a chimney.

there in another car. From the Orange Show Fairgrounds Mr. Wiechert called his wife to tell her that he and the boys were safe.

Later that night the Wiecherts visited the remains of their house. "Nothing was left but a brick wall and the chimney," said John Wiechert. "Everything else had been totally destroyed. Even the aluminum frames of our sliding doors had melted and run into puddles.

"Looking back on it, I feel we could have saved the house if we had stayed," Mr. Wiechert added. "But we left because I feared for the possibility of harm — especially to the kids."

"I had mixed feelings about leaving, too," said Eric Wiechert. "But you always can rebuild a home. You can't rebuild another person."

The Wiecherts did rebuild their house, and they live in it today.

Battalion Chief Fred Poe

At the start of the day, Fred Poe didn't expect that he'd soon be fighting a fire. A battalion chief in the San Bernardino City Fire Department, Poe had fought hundreds of fires in his twenty-nine-year career. But Monday was his day off.

At about eleven-thirty that morning, Poe was contacted and told to take charge of two task forces. Together, the task forces had eighteen fire fighters and six fire engines. Using his two-way radio, Poe told the task forces to go to the northernmost part of the city at the foothills of the San Bernardino Mountains.

"I got there about ten minutes before the first units arrived," Poe remembered. "It was dark and smoky, so I told civilians that they'd better leave. I've seen a lot of brush fires, and I know how people can panic. I told one women who didn't want to leave that she could stay and die or get out and live. She left."

Poe was on the street about half a block from his car when the main body of the fire blew down. "As far ahead of me as I could see, there was nothing but fire. We're trained never to get trapped, always to have an avenue of escape, but this time was different. The fire was burning on a two-mile-wide front, and that wind was blowing it hard."

Knowing that he had to get off the street, the fifty-year-old Poe scrambled over a four-foot-tall backyard wall. He found shelter behind a house. "I got on my hands and knees and kept my head low to get as much air as possible. There was a roar like a blowtorch when the fire went over. Even with my protective clothing and helmet on, it got quite hot. In all my years of fighting fires, I never felt so much danger as in that moment."

Poe huddled behind the house for a couple of minutes until the main body of the firestorm had passed. When he climbed back over the wall, fire fighters and equipment were arriving. Poe got back in his car. Using his two-way radio, he told his men where he wanted them.

"Circumstances were very difficult in fighting this fire," explained Poe. "The wind blew our water streams away. So much water was used that the pressure sometimes fell. The men also were subject to lots of heat, smoke, and dust. Even though we wore goggles, so much dust was flying that just about every fire fighter, including myself, had to go to the hospital later to get his eyes washed out.

The fire fighters shown below were attacking the
fire in the DeVore area on the third day of the fire.

The house still standing had a rock roof. The one next to it had a wooden shake-shingle roof, which caught fire and ignited the rest of the house. Wooden roofs on new buildings are now banned in fire-hazard areas of San Bernardino.

"Because of the wind and the wood-shingle roofs, once a house started on fire it was a lost cause. For example, on one house we were pouring water on a very small square of burning roof. The wind blew so hard that our streams were blown away. That whole house blew up. But we did manage to save some houses that weren't yet on fire by watering down their roofs."

Poe fought the fire for twelve hours before going to the hospital for treatment of his eyes. After his release from the hospital, Poe, like other fire fighters, continued to work for a total of forty-eight hours before he took time to sleep.

Looking back on the fire, Poe says, "It would have made a big difference if people hadn't had those shake-shingle roofs. They're the wrong kind of roof to have in a fire-prone area like Southern California. If not for those roofs, in my opinion there would have been only one-tenth the damage that there was."

After the fire, the city of San Bernardino passed an ordinance banning wooden roofs on new buildings in fire-hazard areas. "We had been harping on the riskiness of those kinds of roofs for years," concluded Poe. "But it often takes some kind of a disaster to make people aware of fire dangers."

3/WHERE DOES FIRE COME FROM?

Well over a million years ago, the first human beings appeared on our planet. The earliest people ate fruits, berries, nuts, and raw meat. They learned to make tools by chipping one stone against another.

At least 500,000 years ago, human beings first used fire. Burned bones and charcoal fragments found in caves prove this. Exactly how fire was discovered is not known. According to one theory, lightning bolts set forests ablaze, and people took burning branches back to their caves. Later, people learned to make their own fires by rubbing sticks together or striking one stone against another to make a spark.

Fire was useful in many ways. It provided warmth during the winter. It lit up caves at night. It was used to cook food, fashion spears, and protect people from wild animals. By firelight people went to the dark recesses of their caves and painted pictures that still can be seen today. By firelight, too, they danced, told stories, and held religious ceremonies.

Fire was just as valuable many years later, when people built the first cities and towns. In ancient Persia, Egypt, and Greece, public fires were kept burning continuously. Guardians made sure that these fires never went out.

Because fire was so valuable, it was an important part of many ancient religions. The Incas of South America used fire in their religious ceremonies. The Romans had a god of fire and metalwork—Vulcan. Vulcan's workshop was said to be deep underground. When the Romans saw a volcano smoking, they said that Vulcan was hard at work making armor and weapons. When a volcano erupted, they said that Vulcan must be angry about something.

The people of many cultures told fire stories. Many of these stories tried to explain how human beings first acquired this useful substance.

The ancient Greeks had an interesting story about the origins of fire. A long time ago, they said, there were no people on earth. A race of gods called Titans ruled the universe. Prometheus, who was one of the Titans, created human beings. Zeus, the king of the gods, did not want people to have fire. But Prometheus felt sorry for the human race. He stole fire from the gods and gave it to humanity. Zeus was enraged. He ordered Prometheus chained to a mountain. There Prometheus remained for thousands of years, while an eagle attacked his body.

The Creek Indians of North America had a more cheerful story. Long ago, they said, people froze during cold weather. One day the Weasels got the gift of fire when lightning struck a tree on their island. The Weasels enjoyed their fire and danced around it, but they wouldn't share it with people. None of the freezing people could swim to the Weasels' island. "I'll get fire for you!" said Rabbit. He put some pine tar in his hair and swam to the island. The Weasels let Rabbit dance with them around the fire. Suddenly Rabbit bent down and let the pine tar in his hair catch fire. He then swam back to the people and gave them their first fire.

The Efik people of Africa said that human beings discovered fire on their own. One day, they said, an old woman wanted to crack open a palm kernel. She put the kernel on a rock and struck at it with a big knife. The knife missed the kernel, but it hit the stone and created a spark. At that moment the Efik people were introduced to fire.

Although fire provided much that was good, even ancient people knew that it could be very harmful. A fire in Rome in

The Great London Fire of 1666 burned down most of the city and left 200,000 people homeless.

the year 12 B.C. prompted the Emperor Augustus to form one of the world's first fire departments. Nevertheless, another huge fire devastated Rome in the year 64 A.D. This was the fire in which the Emperor Nero supposedly "fiddled while Rome burned."

Many cities have been completely or partially destroyed by fire. During a war in 1571, as many as 170,000 people died when Moscow, Russia was set ablaze. In 1666 a fire that began in a bakery in Pudding Lane burned down most of London. In 1729 a fire killed 7,000 people and destroyed much of Constantinople (now Istanbul, Turkey). One of the worst fire storms of all time occurred during World War II, when the German city of Dresden was firebombed. More than 135,000 people died.

American cities have suffered from huge fires, too. In 1607 the English formed their first permanent settlement in America at Jamestown, Virginia. Less than a year later, a big fire destroyed much of Jamestown. In 1676 Jamestown was burned to the ground during a revolt against the royal governor.

This 1872 fire in Boston killed fourteen people and destroyed hundreds of buildings.

Just about every major city in the United States has suffered from a devastating fire. A 1788 blaze burned down four-fifths of New Orleans. A bad fire in New York City burned down 650 buildings in 1835. One of Boston's worst fires, in 1872, killed fourteen people and destroyed 547 buildings. On July 4, 1866, a boy in Portland, Maine threw a firecracker into a stack of wood shavings. The fire that resulted burned down half the city. In 1906 an earthquake that struck San Francisco ignited fires that burned down much of the city.

Fires can be started in many ways. Lightning, earthquakes, and volcanoes ignite some blazes. People, however, are responsible for most of the fires that occur in the world today. Careless human beings start fires with matches and cigarettes, furnaces and stoves, firecrackers and bombs.

What Happens When a Fire Starts

A fire is the heat, light, and flame produced by burning materials. To start a fire, three things are needed. The first requirement is *fuel*—something that will burn. The second necessity is *heat* to set the fuel afire. Third, *oxygen* (which is found in air) is needed to keep the fire going.

If you've ever watched someone barbecue, you've seen the three elements of a fire at work. The coals and pieces of wood in the barbecue are the fuel. A match usually provides the heat needed to start the fire. The air surrounding the barbecue provides the oxygen to keep the fire going.

If any one of those three elements is missing, the barbecue can't produce a lasting fire. Without coals or wood for fuel, the chef can't even think of starting a fire. If there are no matches or other sources of heat, the chef is out of luck. If a fire is started but then deprived of oxygen by being covered or drowned with water, the fire will go out.

When fire fighters battle a blaze, they try to deprive it of one or more of the three elements a fire needs to burn. They pour water on fires to take away the heat. They spray chemical foams on fires to cut them off from oxygen. They turn off gas supplies, build firebreaks, and start backfires to cut blazes off from their fuel.

How Fires Kill

Just as in the days of cave people, fire is still very useful to human beings. We use it to cook our food and heat our homes. Fire runs the steam turbines that generate electricity. It is used in mills to make steel, and in refineries to make gasoline.

Smoke is the main killer in fires.

But fires help us only when they are planned and under control. Unplanned, uncontrolled fires burn down our buildings. They destroy our forests. Worst of all, they kill people.

Fire kills in several ways. Smoke is the main killer. Every person on earth needs to breathe oxygen. When people breathe in smoke instead of oxygen, they choke, gasp, and eventually suffocate. A person who has died from smoke or been injured by it is said to have suffered *smoke inhalation.*

Smoke is particularly deadly in a nightime fire because it tends to put people to sleep rather than wake them up. Smoke rises and travels quickly. Therefore, it can kill people in different rooms or even on different floors from the actual fire.

The flames and tremendous heat of a fire also are deadly. In some fires the temperature tops 1,500° F. People are burned to death.

4/SOME FAMOUS FIRES

Smoke, heat, and flames are the main killers in both small and big fires. In this chapter you will see these killers at work in some famous fires.

Peshtigo, Wisconsin, 1871 -
The Deadliest Fire in American History

The summer of 1871 was hot and dry. In northeastern Wisconsin, little rain fell during the month of July. In August there was no rain at all, and in September there was only a drizzle.When the animals of the forest went down to the streams for drinking water, they found the streambeds dry. People lowered buckets into their wells only to find that the wells had dried up, too.

By early fall, many small fires were burning in the forests and swamps of northern Wisconsin. These fires had started by themselves (by a process called *spontaneous combustion*) because of the extreme dryness.

The 1871 fire in the forest near Peshtigo, Wisconsin spread so rapidly that many families were stranded in clearings.

The people of Peshtigo fled to the river to escape the heat and flames.

On Sunday, October 8, smoke could be smelled in
Peshtigo, a booming lumber town of two thousand people in
northeastern Wisconsin. "Fire's somewhere close!" said the
people of Peshtigo on their way home from church. As the
day went on, the forest fire came closer and closer. Ashes
floated down from the sky.

Confused birds circled over the town and frightened forest
animals ran through the streets. To the south, the sky turned
red. Even before flames could be seen, the heat in Peshtigo
was so great that people soaked rags in the Peshtigo River and

dripped the water over their faces. By early evening the loud, continuous roar of the fire could be heard. The people could do nothing but hope that it would miss their town.

The fire reached Peshtigo at about nine in the evening. First the tops of the trees on the outskirts of town caught fire. Like a great meteor shower, sparks flared down on Peshtigo and started more fires. Some people ran about trying to beat out the flames. But the blaze had become a truly monstrous fire storm that could not be stopped.

Flaming roofs tore loose from houses and went sailing through the air. Tree limbs flew through the sky like fiery spears. Everywhere the people turned, they saw fire.

Some terrified people remained inside buildings, which soon became death traps. It wasn't just the flames that were deadly. The fire consumed so much oxygen that there wasn't enough left for people to breathe.

Some people made their way down to the river and jumped in. Even in the water, the people of Peshtigo weren't safe. Some were struck by flaming pieces of wood. Others were felled by waves of heat and gas when they came up to breathe.

All through the night the survivors watched the flames consume their town. At dawn, they found that Peshtigo no longer existed. Of the town's four hundred buildings, all that remained was the wall of one house.

Approximately fifteen hundred people had died in and around Peshtigo, making this the deadliest fire ever to strike the United States. Countless forest and farm animals also had been killed.

Terrible as it was, the Peshtigo Fire did not receive much attention in the newpapers of the time. That was because another deadly fire struck on the very same day — a fire that destroyed much of a major city.

The Great Chicago Fire · 1871

Chicago, 250 miles south of Peshtigo, suffered through the same dry summer of 1871. Unlike Peshtigo, Chicago was a very large city. With 335,000 people, it was the fourth largest city in the United States.

In Peshtigo the danger of fire came from the surrounding forest. In Chicago, the main danger lay in the fact that most of the city was made of wood. Houses, fences, bridges—even the sidewalks—were wooden. To make things worse, many of Chicago's wooden structures had been built quickly, without considering fire safety. Buildings were too close together. Streets were too narrow. Because of these conditions, small fires easily grew into big ones.

Chicago's fire fighters battled blazes throughout the summer and early fall of 1871. In the first week of October, they squelched thirty fires. A big one on October 7-8 destroyed several blocks of lumber yards, factories, and houses. It took Chief Fire Marshal Robert A. Williams and his crew sixteen hours to put out that blaze, which was Chicago's worst fire up to that time.

Left: Robert A. Williams, chief of the Chicago Fire Department in 1871.
Below: An 1858 photograph taken from the Court House dome shows the crowded wooden structures that made up the city of Chicago before the Great Chicago Fire.

Mrs. Kate O'Leary's house at 137 De Koven Street

By Sunday afternoon, October 8, 1871, Chief Williams and his fire fighters were exhausted. Williams was worried. Many times he had asked for more workers and equipment. But city officials had said that 185 fire fighters and 17 horse-drawn fire engines were enough. After the big weekend fire, Williams didn't have even that many workers or engines. Sixty of his fire crew, suffering from smoke inhalation or burns, had been sent to the hospital. Several engines were broken. What would the fire department do if there were another big fire?

On the evening of October 8, Chief Williams asked his wife to awaken him if the city's fire bells were rung. Hoping that his department wouldn't be needed that night, he went to sleep.

While Williams slept, a fire broke out in a barn at 137 De Koven Street, on the city's Southwest Side. The fire might have started when Kate O'Leary's cow kicked over a kerosene lamp. Soon the barn was ablaze. It was a windy evening, and the fire spread to the surrounding structures.

The first alarm was given from Goll's Drugstore (right), but the alarm system wasn't working so the fire department did not receive the message.

To keep a small fire from growing, fire fighters must put it out quickly. Unfortunately, it took many minutes for a crew to reach the scene. Everything went wrong. A man in a nearby drugstore pulled the fire alarm. But the message never got to headquarters because the alarm system wasn't working. When the department's fire spotters noticed the flames, they rang the city's fire bells. But they sent the engines to the wrong place. By the time the main body of fire fighters arrived, two square blocks were ablaze.

For a while, Chief Williams and his company thought they could contain the fire. But the blaze developed into a fire storm. The wind picked up burning pieces of wood and hurled them through the air. A flaming piece of wood was hurled half a mile to the steeple of St. Paul's Church. In

FIRST CLASS DOUBLE ENGINE, WITH ONE ROTARY PUMP.

The Little Giant (left) was the first fire engine to reach Mrs. O'Leary's house on De Koven Street. Right: A fireman shouts orders as fire fighters work to control the fire, which had spread rapidly.

minutes the entire church was ablaze. The flames leaped from St. Paul's to the lumber yard next door. Soon there were so many fires in so many places that the fire crews were virtually helpless.

There was great danger when flames approached the gasworks. The mixture of fire and gas could set off a terrible explosion. With Chief Williams at his side, the superintendent of the gasworks let the gas out of the tanks. Some of the gas was pumped into reserve tanks. The rest went into the city's sewers. The gasworks didn't explode. But every time a spark landed near a sewer, there was an explosion.

Much of Chicago was now lit up by orange and yellow flames. It was said that a person twenty miles from the fire could read a newspaper in the light of the blaze.

Huge crowds tried to flee the flames by crossing the Randolph Street bridge.

At two-thirty in the morning the flames leaped across the Chicago River and began to burn the city's North Side. People who were crossing the river on bridges jumped into the water to escape the flames. Some of them drowned.

Thousands made their way to the shores of Lake Michigan. They waded out into the water. Even there, the heat was so intense that people's hair was burned.

At about three in the morning, the city's waterworks caught fire. The fire fighters no longer had water to continue their feeble stand against the flames. On Monday, October 9, the fire continued to burn the North Side. Finally, it began to run out of fuel. Rain squelched the last flames.

Above: The Crosby Opera House burns during the Great Fire.
Below: This view from Lake Michigan shows Chicago at
the height of the fire as flames consume the city on
both sides of the Chicago River.

A view of Chicago after the fire

The Great Chicago Fire was one of the worst disasters ever to hit a major American city. Nearly twenty thousand houses and other buildings had burned down. Approximately a hundred thousand persons were left homeless. The worst part was that at least three hundred people were killed.

"CHICAGO SHALL RISE AGAIN" proclaimed a Chicago newspaper. The paper was right. In the months and years that followed, more people moved into the city. New buildings were constructed. Just thirteen years after the fire, the world's first skyscraper went up in Chicago. Skyscrapers and other new buildings were made of iron, steel, and concrete. Such buildings were less likely to catch fire than wooden ones.

Every year, the people of the United States and Canada observe National Fire Prevention Week. During that week, schoolchildren learn how to protect themselves and their homes from fire. National Fire Prevention Week is held in early October, on the anniversary of the Great Chicago Fire.

The Bigelow House, a new hotel that was to have opened its doors on October 9, was in ruins after the fire (above). Chicago's Water Tower (below) was one of the few buildings that survived. It stands today as a reminder of the Great Chicago Fire.

The General Slocum Disaster · 1904

June 15, 1904 was supposed to be a joyous day for the people of St. Mark's German Lutheran Church in New York City. It was the day of their yearly Sunday School picnic. Early on that Wednesday morning, hundreds of people walked from the church to the East River Pier on Third Street. They boarded a steamboat named the *General Slocum.* The boat was to take them up the East River to Locust Grove, Long Island. There they would eat their picnic lunches. After the picnic, the boat would return them to New York City.

The *General Slocum* was one of the most impressive pleasure boats that docked in New York Harbor. It was 250 feet long and had three decks. As the huge vessel left the harbor, none of the 1,358 passengers or crew of 23 could have guessed that disaster was about to strike.

Inside the ship, a cook was making clam chowder for the picnic. Smoke came from the stove. Shortly after the trip began, a boy noticed some additional smoke coming from a storage room. He told the captain.

Captain William Van Schaick ignored the boy. Perhaps the captain thought that the smoke was coming from the stove. Or perhaps he thought the boy was making up a story. By ignoring him, Captain Van Schaick gave the fire time to grow.

A crewman on a river dredge also saw smoke spiraling upward from the *General Slocum.* He blew the whistle four times to signal danger. A fireboat, the *Zophar Mills,* began to chase the burning vessel. Some police officers and fire fighters hurried into small boats and also gave chase.

As people yelled, "The ship's on fire!" the captain realized that the boy had been right. There were places along the East River where Captain Van Schaick could have let the people off the burning ship. But the captain made what proved to be a terrible decision. He headed toward North Brother Island, about three miles away. Meanwhile, he hoped that his crew could put out the flames.

When people feel heat and see flames, they tend to panic. That is why fire drills are important. Fire drills teach people to do the right thing automatically, no matter how afraid or confused they may be. The captain and crew of the *General Slocum* had never had a fire drill. To make things worse, their equipment was in terrible condition. When the fire hose was taken out, it crumbled.

As the flames spread through the wooden ship, some passengers' clothes caught fire. Seeing that they had to jump from the ship, people grabbed life preservers. Like the water hose, the preservers were in bad condition. Many fell to pieces immediately.

Even without life preservers, people jumped into the river. A few were picked up by the boats that were pursuing the *General Slocum.* Reverend George Haas, the pastor of the church, later described the scene in the water:

> In three minutes—it could not have been more—all three decks were ablaze. . . . With my wife and daughter I went overboard. I do not know whether we jumped or whether we were pushed over. When I rose to the top of the water I saw scores and scores of people fighting to keep afloat, and then one by one they would sink for the last time. It was awful and I was powerless to do anything. I did not see my wife or daughter.

Finally, with flames leaping sixty feet above its decks, the *General Slocum* reached North Brother Island. The boats that had followed the burning ship rescued some people. Doctors and nurses from a hospital on the island swam out and rescued others. But even at the edge of the island, dozens were burned to death and dozens more drowned.

The General Slocum

The deck of the
General Slocum *was
strewn with debris
after the tragic fire.*

Of the 1,381 people who had been aboard the *General Slocum,* 1,030 perished. The cause of the fire was never definitely learned.

After this disaster, fire drills became a regular part of passenger-ship crew training. Emergency items such as fire hoses and life preservers were checked more closely. Unfortunately, it took this terrible disaster to put such common-sense safety measures into practice.

Fire Over Japan - The Earthquake of 1923

As noon approached on September 1, 1923, the people of Japan were preparing lunch. At 11:58 A.M. the earth began to rumble. *"Jishin!"* ("Earthquake!") people shouted. Japan has so many quakes that it has been nicknamed "The World's Earthquake Factory." But this quake was monstrous. In the cities of Tokyo and Yokohama, buildings collapsed like toys.

Toppling stoves caused many of the falling buildings to catch fire. Blown by strong winds, the flames leaped from building to building. With water mains broken in many places, fire fighters couldn't get water to fight the flames. Soon the cities of Tokyo and Yokohama were ablaze.

In many places people couldn't get to safety because of large crowds and narrow streets.

Even in open places, people weren't safe from the flames. In Tokyo, more than 40,000 persons sought refuge in an open park that served as the Military Clothing Depot. The buildings surrounding the park caught fire, sending a fire storm through the crowd at 150 miles per hour. At least 38,000 people died in that one location.

In Tokyo, 134 separate fires destroyed 400,000 buildings. In Yokohama, two-thirds of all the buildings were destroyed by the earthquake and fires. Few of the blazes were put out by fire fighters. The flames raged on until they had no more fuel to consume.

The final death toll from this disaster was approximately 143,000. In Tokyo alone 100,000 persons were killed. Most of the dead—no one knows exactly how many—had perished in the fires.

The Japanese people learned some lessons from this horrible disaster. They widened their streets so that people would have room to flee during earthquakes. They also designed new water mains to withstand large shocks. This planning has helped. Japan has been rocked by many earthquakes in the past sixty years. But none has been nearly so deadly as the earthquake of 1923.

In 1812, Emperor Napoleon of France raised an army to march against Russia. By the time Napoleon reached Moscow, the few Russians left in that city had set fire to it, leaving for Napoleon nothing but ruins.

SOME MAJOR FIRES OUTSIDE THE UNITED STATES

Date	Place	Description	Estimated Deaths
64 A.D.	Rome, Italy	Fire burned for eight days.	Not known
1571	Moscow, Russia	The city was burned during wartime.	Reportedly 170,000
September, 2-6, 1666	London, England	The "Great London Fire" left 200,000 homeless.	Only four known
1729	Constantinople (now Istanbul, Turkey)	The worst of many fires in this city.	7,000
September 14, 1812	Moscow, Russia	This wartime fire burned down most of the city.	Not known
February 14, 1836	St. Petersburg, Russia	Fire in a theater.	700
May, 1845	Canton, China	Fire in a theater.	More than 1,600
December 8, 1863	Santiago, Chile	Fire in a church.	At least 2,000
December 8, 1881	Vienna, Austria	Fire in the Ring Theater.	At least 640
September 1, 1923	Japan	Much of Tokyo and Yokohama were destroyed by earthquake and fires.	143,000 (Most died in the fires.)
March 22, 1934	Hakodate, Japan	The city was destroyed by fire.	More than 2,000
November 14, 1939	Lagunillas, Venezuela	Fire that started in an oil refinery.	More than 500
July-August, 1943	Hamburg, Germany	Fire storm from Allied bombing during World War II.	More than 50,000
February 13-15, 1945	Dresden, Germany	Fire storm from more Allied bombing.	More than 135,000
March, 1945	Tokyo, Japan	U.S. firebombed the city during World War II.	84,000
September 2, 1949	Chungking, China	Fire left 100,000 homeless.	1,700
December 17, 1961	Niterói, Brazil	Fire in a circus tent.	323
August 20, 1978	Abadan, Iran	Arsonists set fire to a theater.	Nearly 400
May 20, 1980	Kingston, Jamaica	Fire in a wooden home for the poor.	More than 150

SOME MAJOR UNITED STATES FIRES

Date	Place	Description	Estimated Deaths
January 7, 1608	Jamestown, Virginia	Much of the first permanent English settlement in America burned.	*
March 21, 1788	New Orleans, Louisiana	Fire destroyed more than 850 buildings.	*
August, 1814	Washington, D.C.	During the War of 1812, the English burned the White House, the Capitol, and other government offices.	*
December 16, 1835	New York City, New York	Fire burned 650 buildings.	None
November, 1864-Spring, 1865	Southern United States	During the Civil War, Northern soldiers burned Atlanta, Columbia, and other Southern cities.	Not known
July 4, 1866	Portland, Maine	Fire ignited by a boy playing with fireworks destroyed half the city.	None
October 8, 1871	In and around Peshtigo, Wisconsin	Forest Fire.	1,500
October 8, 1871	Chicago, Illinois	"Great Chicago Fire" burned nearly 20,000 buildings.	At least 300
November 9, 1872	Boston, Massachusetts	Fire destroyed 547 buildings.	14
December 5, 1876	Brooklyn, New York	Theater fire.	More than 300
September 1, 1894	Hinckley, Minnesota	Forest Fire.	418
June 30, 1900	Hoboken, New Jersey	Ship and dock fire.	326
September 20, 1902	Birmingham, Alabama	Fire in a church.	115
December 30, 1903	Chicago, Illinois	Fire in the Iroquois Theater.	639
June 15, 1904	New York City, New York	Fire on the excursion boat General Slocum.	1,030
April 18, 1906	San Francisco, California	Earthquake, followed by fires.	700 (Mostly from the fires.)
November 13, 1909	Cherry, Illinois	Fire in a coal mine.	259
March 25, 1911	New York City, New York	Fire in the Triangle Shirtwaist Factory.	145

* None, or very few.

October, 1918	Minnesota and Wisconsin	Forest fires.	1,000
April 21, 1930	Columbia, Ohio	Fire in the Ohio State Penitentiary.	320
April 23, 1940	Natchez, Mississippi	Fire in a dance hall.	198
November 28, 1942	Boston, Massachusetts	Fire in the Cocoanut Grove nightclub.	499
July 6, 1944	Hartford, Connecticut	Fire in a circus tent.	168
December 7, 1946	Atlanta, Georgia	Fire in the Winecoff Hotel.	119
December 1, 1958	Chicago, Illinois	Fire in Our Lady of Angels School.	95
May 2, 1972	Kellogg, Idaho	Fire in a silver mine.	91
May 28, 1977	Southgate, Kentucky	Fire in a supper club.	167
November 21, 1980	Las Vegas, Nevada	Hotel fire.	84

Firemen battle an 1861 fire in Washington, D.C.

5/EXPLOSIONS

When fire burns very rapidly, violent expansion of gases often causes an *explosion*. Explosions produce tremendous amounts of heat and energy and can be deadly. Some of the most violent explosions have occurred in mines, on ships, and in places where gunpowder and other explosives were stored. One of history's worst accidental explosions occurred in 1856, when lightning struck a church on the Greek island of Rhodes. Gunpowder stored in the church exploded, killing four thousand people.

The deadliest explosions have been set on purpose, during times of war. By 1945 United States scientists knew how to produce an atomic explosion by splitting the cores of atoms. They created the atomic bomb. It was capable of producing a giant fireball hotter than the surface of the sun. When the United States dropped two atomic bombs on Japan in 1945, more than 132,000 people were killed.

The deadliest explosion in North American history also occurred during wartime.

The Halifax Disaster - 1917

In the year 1917 World War I was raging. On one side were the Central Powers, which included Germany and Austria-Hungary. On the other side were the Allies, which included the United States, France, England, and Canada.

Halifax, a city in the Canadian province of Nova Scotia, was headquarters for the Allied ships that sailed between North America and Europe.

On the morning of December 6, 1917, a French ship, the *Mont Blanc,* entered Halifax Harbor. On the ship were 450,000 tons of the explosive TNT. The ship also carried 2,300 tons of explosive picric acid and 35 tons of flammable benzol.

The *Mont Blanc* was supposed to join a ship convoy in Halifax. Then it would head for Europe, where it would deliver the explosives to the Allied armies. But as the *Mont Blanc* entered the narrow part of the harbor, it approached another ship, the Norwegian freighter *Imo.* Despite last-second efforts to avoid a collision, the ships smashed into each other.

The jolt set some of the benzol aflame on the *Mont Blanc.* The blazing fuel ran across the deck of the ship. The captain of the *Mont Blanc* knew that once the flames reached the TNT, there would be a horrible explosion. "Abandon ship!" he ordered. The crew of the *Mont Blanc* got into lifeboats and rowed for shore.

Just a few minutes after the sailors abandoned the *Mont Blanc,* the ship exploded. It was one of the most violent explosions in history. The *Mont Blanc* was blown to smithereens. A 1,000-pound piece of the ship's anchor was sent flying three miles through the air. Metal pieces of the ship were hurled more than a mile before falling to the ground. Where the ship had once been, a gigantic black cloud could be seen mushrooming six hundred feet into the sky.

The blast wave of the explosion ripped through Halifax like a volcanic eruption. The heat was so intense that fires were ignited, burning people inside their homes. The shock created large waves in the harbor that drowned people near the shore. The blast also sent people, animals, cars, glass, and trees flying through the air. Telephone poles a mile from the blast were blown out of the ground, and windows were shattered at a distance of more than a hundred miles.

At a school the walls caved in, killing two hundred children. A church and railroad station also collapsed, killing people inside. The streets of Halifax were filled with screaming, crying, bleeding people.

In the minutes following the blast, Halifax was vulnerable to more explosions. A British ship, the *Picton,* lay close to where the *Mont Blanc* had been. The *Picton* was on fire. The captain and most of the crew were dead. The rest of the crew had fled. Loaded with explosives, the *Picton* could blow up at any second.

Captain J.W. Harrison went out to the *Picton.* He cut the ship loose so that it would float away from the city. He then let in some seawater and sprayed water on the fire until its flames went out.

Back in Halifax, half the city lay in ruins. More than sixteen hundred people were dead. Eight thousand were injured. More than ten thousand people had lost their homes.

Who was at fault for this disaster? Some blamed the *Mont Blanc* for the collision and explosion. Others said that the *Imo* should have sped out of the way. Still others said that explosives and highly flammable materials shouldn't be brought so close to a city.

Perhaps the war itself should have received the brunt of the blame. Explosions, both accidental and purposeful, have always been a hazard of war.

These temporary apartments housed fifteen hundred to eighteen hundred persons made homeless by the explosion of the Mont Blanc *in Halifax Harbor.*

After the explosion, the Halifax Harbor area was in ruins (above).
The warehouse pictured below helped supply goods necessary for the
relief of the thousands of Halifax people who were left homeless.

Coal mine explosion and fire near Manchester, England

SOME MAJOR EXPLOSIONS OUTSIDE THE UNITED STATES

Date	Place	Description	Estimated Deaths
1769	Brescia, Italy	Explosion of gunpowder stored in an arsenal.	3,000
1856	Island of Rhodes, Greece	Lightning struck a church, causing gunpowder stored there to explode.	4,000
March 10, 1906	Courrières, France	Explosion in a mine.	1,060
December 6, 1917	Halifax, Nova Scotia, Canada	Explosion of an ammunition ship.	More than 1,600
September 21, 1921	Oppau, Germany	Explosion in a chemical plant.	More than 1,000
April 26, 1942	Honkeiko, Manchuria, China	Mine explosion.	More than 1,500
April 9, 1945	Bari, Italy	American ship loaded with bombs exploded.	360
August 6, 1945	Hiroshima, Japan	U.S. exploded an atomic bomb on the city during World War II.	More than 92,000
August 9, 1945	Nagasaki, Japan	Second atomic bomb was dropped by the U.S. on Japan.	At least 40,000
August 18, 1947	Cádiz, Spain	Explosion at a naval torpedo factory.	400
July 28, 1948	Ludwigshafen, West Germany	Chemical company explosion.	200
August 7, 1956	Cali, Colombia	Trucks carrying dynamite exploded.	1,100
June 23, 1958	Santo Amaro, Brazil	Explosion of fireworks.	100
March 4, 1960	Havana, Cuba	Ammunition ship exploded.	More than 100
July 23, 1964	Bone, Algeria	Ammunition ship exploded.	100
July 29, 1967	Off Vietnam coast	Fire and explosions on U.S. aircraft carrier *Forrestal*.	134
June 6, 1972	Wankie, Rhodesia	Explosion in a coal mine.	427
December 27, 1975	Dhanbad, India	Explosion and then flooding of a mine.	More than 400

SOME MAJOR UNITED STATES EXPLOSIONS

Date	Place	Description	Estimated Deaths
May 1, 1900	Scofield, Utah	Explosion of blasting powder in a mine.	200
January 25, 1904	Cheswick, Utah	Explosion in a coal mine.	179
December 6, 1907	Monongah, West Virginia	Explosion in a coal mine.	362
December 19, 1907	Jacobs Creek, Pennsylvania	Explosion in a mine.	239
October 22, 1913	Dawson, New Mexico	Explosion in a coal mine.	263
April 10, 1917	Eddystone, Pennsylvania	Munitions plant explosion.	133
May 19, 1928	Mather, Pennsylvania	Explosion in a coal mine.	195
May 15, 1929	Cleveland, Ohio	Explosion in a medical facility set fire to X-ray film, releasing poisonous fumes.	125
March 18, 1937	New London, Texas	Explosion in a school.	413
May 6, 1937	Lakehurst, New Jersey	Explosion and fire on airship *Hindenburg*.	36
July 17, 1944	Port Chicago, California	Explosion of ammunition ships.	322
October 20, 1944	Cleveland, Ohio	Explosion of liquid-gas tanks.	More than 125
April 16, 1947	Texas City, Texas	Explosion of the ship *Grandcamp* destroyed much of the city.	468
December 21, 1951	West Frankfort, Illinois	Explosion in a coal mine.	119
December 22, 1977	Westwego, Louisiana	Explosion in a grain company plant.	36

In 1865, an explosion caused this fire at the Mobile, Alabama waterfront.

6/PROTECTING YOURSELF FROM FIRE

Each year, approximately 7,000 people in the United States die in fires. That's enough people to populate a town. Each year thirty times as many Americans die in fires as in tornadoes, floods, and hurricanes combined. The 200,000 people who are injured in fires each year add to the grim statistics. Some are burned so badly that they are permanently scarred or crippled.

If you read the newspaper or watch the news on television, you will learn about the most spectacular fires. For example, a 1977 fire in a Kentucky supper club made the headlines because it killed 167 persons. The Las Vegas hotel fire that killed 84 people in 1980 was another big news story. Such large-scale disasters are rare. Of the 7,000 yearly deaths, most occur in one- and two-family home fires that never make the headlines.

The tragic fact about fire deaths is that practically all of them are unnecessary. A few fires are ignited by lightning. But almost all of the 2½ million fires reported yearly in the United States are caused by carelessness or recklessness.

Approximately 75,000 fires per year are caused by children playing with matches. Usually the children don't intend to start a fire. They're just curious. Nevertheless, many of the fires they start burn down buildings and kill people. Adults who are careless with cigarettes also start approximately 75,000 fires per year. A forgotten or discarded cigarette can burn for almost half an hour. That gives it plenty of time to set a bed or couch—and then a whole house—on fire.

There are many other causes of fires besides matches and cigarettes. Faulty electrical wiring, carelessness while

*A few fires are ignited
by lightning, but most
are caused by
carelessness or recklessness.*

cooking, and unsafe heating systems are three leading causes. Some people even start fires on purpose—often to collect insurance money. Those who do that have committed arson, a very serious crime.

The United States has no single set of fire laws. There are nearly 20,000 separate sets of laws for various localities. In many cities, public buildings are required to have smoke detectors, sprinkler systems, and fire alarms. There are also codes and standards about the materials used in the construction of private homes and apartments. Once a residence has been built, however, fire safety is mainly the job of those who live there.

Fire Prevention in Your House or Apartment

About 80 percent of the yearly fire deaths in the United States occur in houses and apartments. No one can guarantee that you will never have a fire where you live. But fire experts agree that families who are aware of potential fire hazards can do much to avoid such a blaze.

Stay away from matches or cigarette lighters. They should be used by adults only. If you see a child handling matches, warn an adult.

If anyone in your home falls asleep with a cigarette—or leaves a cigarette burning—awaken him or her immediately.

Make sure that children stay away from appliances that can start fires. Any person too young to cook should not go near the stove, toaster, or other electrical appliances. Let adults operate them.

Make sure that electrical cords in your home are in good condition. Worn-out cords may spark and start a fire.

Do not put too many plugs in one outlet. That can overload a circuit and heat up the wires inside a wall and start a fire.

Stay away from fire. You don't ever want your clothes to catch fire. So if someone is cooking on the backyard grill, don't get too close to the fire. If you have a fireplace, stay away from the flames.

Do not open or handle containers of flammable or combustible material. The words *flammable* or *combustible* warn that the contents can easily catch fire. If you see a flammable or combustible container near a fire, tell an adult about it. Safe storage of these containers—in a garage, for instance—will reduce the fire hazards.

Don't store piles of materials that burn easily. Fire needs fuel to keep burning. Piles of old newspapers, rags, or personal belongings make excellent fuel. A cigarette dropped in a pile of old newspapers has caused many a blaze. By helping to keep your home neat, you are helping to prevent fires.

Keep items that can burn away from stoves or heaters.

Keep Christmas trees away from any heat source.

Keep a screen in front of your fireplace.

Have the fireplace chimney cleaned regularly.

Have your furnace or other source of heat checked and cleaned regularly.

On Halloween, wear costumes made of materials that won't burn, and be careful with the candles in the jack-o-lanterns.

Smoke Detectors and Home Fire Drills

Even after people have taken every reasonable precaution, it is still possible for fires to start in a house or apartment. For that reason, fire experts suggest that *smoke detectors* be put up on every level of a home or apartment building. The safest way is to have a smoke detector in or near every sleeping area. Smoke detectors sound warnings when smoke begins to fill a room. This warning awakens sleeping people who might otherwise be overcome by smoke.

You should know what to do when a fire occurs. That is why experts suggest that families conduct *fire drills.*

First, your family should sit down and figure out all the escape routes in your house or apartment. You should have at least two ways out of your home—the front and back doors. You also may have more than one way to get out of each room. For example, if your bedroom is on a ground floor, you should be able to get out through a window in case of fire. Knowing all the escape exits is the first step of the drills.

WHERE THERE'S SMOKE... THERE SHOULD BE A SMOKE ALARM.

IT'S ONE SURE WAY TO GET OUT OF THE HOUSE IN TIME.

Smoke detectors like those shown below can awaken sleeping people and save lives.

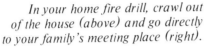
In your home fire drill, crawl out of the house (above) and go directly to your family's meeting place (right).

Next, your family should agree on a meeting place outside your home. Decide on a place where all would meet in case of a real fire. It could be a neighbor's home or a lamppost or a tree in front of your own home.

To start your family fire drills, everyone should go into his or her bedroom and close the door. Somebody can whistle to start each drill. You'll do a lot of pretending in your drills.

In this case, pretend that the whistle is the sound of a smoke alarm or a cry of "Fire!"

- *Drill One:* As soon as you hear the alarm, go to your door. Feel it. Pretend that the door is cool. That means there probably is no fire outside the door. But pretend your home is filled with heat. Heat and smoke rise. The closer you are to the floor, the better the air is and the safer you are. So *crawl* out of your bedroom and then out of your home. Do not stop for pets, toys, or important papers. In a real fire, you wouldn't even stop to call the fire department. Once out of the house, go directly to your family's meeting place. If this were a real fire, someone in your family would then call the fire department.

- *Drill Two:* Pretend that your bedroom door is very hot. The heat could mean there is a fire right outside your door. Don't open that door—the flames would burn you! In this case, go out by your alternate route—perhaps through a window if you live on a ground floor. Even if you have no way out of your room, you can still save yourself. Place sheets or blankets at the bottom of the door. That will keep the smoke out. Then *crawl* to the window so you can get some air. To let fire fighters know you are there, hang a sheet or a bedspread out the window.

You may not want to climb out the window or hang out sheets during this drill. But you should remember that someday you may have to climb out a window or place sheets at the bottom of a door to keep a fire out.

What to Do in a Real Fire

You may never have to face an uncontrolled fire. But the United States Fire Administration says that each American is likely to be involved in fires requiring the fire department three times during his or her lifetime. If you find yourself in a big fire, knowing what to do can save your life. Here is some advice from experts for times of real fires. It covers some of the actions you practiced in your drills.

- Go to your door and feel it to see if it's hot.

- If the door isn't hot, leave the room and then the building. Leave immediately and don't come back. If you encounter smoke while leaving, drop down to the floor and crawl out.

- If the door is hot when you feel it, go out through the window or another route. If you have no way to get out, keep your door closed so that smoke can't get into the room. Drop down to the floor, where the fresher air is, and crawl over to the window. Open it and hang a sheet or a blanket out the window to alert firemen that you are in the room.

- If your clothes catch fire, don't run. Stand still, then drop to the floor and roll around. That will help put out the flames. Fire experts call this action *stop, drop, and roll.* You should do it any time your clothes catch fire.

- Once out of your building, do not return for any reason. Call the fire department from a location that is a safe distance from the fire.

The United States' Fire Departments

Back in America's early years, church bells rang out a series
of short taps when there was a fire. Volunteers rushed out of
their homes and formed ''bucket brigades''—two lines of fire
fighters. One line passed water-filled buckets, which were
dumped on the fire. The empty buckets were passed back
along the second row and then refilled. Bucket brigades
provided a small but continuous supply of water.

One of the colonists' first attempts at providing fire alarms
was made in 1658 by Peter Stuyvesant. As governor of what is
now the state of New York, Stuyvesant put eight men on
patrol in New York City from sundown to sunrise. When they

A bucket brigade at work during a frontier village fire

spotted a fire they shook rattles to warn people. Because of that they were called the "Rattle Watch."

The first paid fire department in what is now the United States was formed in Boston in 1679. In Philadelphia in 1736, Benjamin Franklin was the first to organize a group of volunteers as a department. Franklin also started the first fire insurance company in the United States.

Today, the United States has thousands of fire departments. Most big cities have paid departments. Fire fighting is their full-time work. Many small towns have volunteer fire departments. People belonging to these departments usually have other jobs. They are called upon when a fire breaks out in the town.

Benjamin Franklin (left) was the first person to organize a group of volunteers as a fire department. George Washington (above) donated a fire engine to Friendship Company of Alexandria, Virginia.

This Currier and Ives lithograph shows early fire-fighting equipment being rushed to the scene of a fire.

Another Currier and Ives lithograph shows a hand pumper being pulled out of its barn by volunteer firemen.

Today's city fire departments have a variety of modern equipment and highly trained fire fighters.

Smoke jumpers parachute from airplanes to fight fires (above).
Helicopters rescue people from burning buildings. The one shown here was used to rescue people from the burning MGM Grand Hotel in Las Vegas on November 21, 1980. This was the second worst hotel blaze in United States history.

Big fire departments have a variety of modern equipment at their disposal. Today's *fire trucks* can pump hundreds of gallons of water per minute. *Fireboats* go out onto rivers and lakes to fight blazes along the shore. *Helicopters* rescue people from burning buildings. The United States Forest Service even employs *smoke jumpers,* who parachute from airplanes to fight forest fires.

Your fire department will respond if you call them about a fire. They will put out the blaze and rescue people who may be trapped in the building. Many fire departments will also send out experts to help your family check its home fire safety. They may even help your family with its fire drill.

You can be just as helpful to your fire department as they are to you. Every fire you read about in this book could have been harmless—if it had been put out soon enough. Learn your fire department's telephone number. If you see a fire anywhere, call the fire department right away. If you see someone committing the crime of arson, call the fire department at once. By taking such action, you may save someone's life.

*Above: Moscow in flames in 1812
Right: The Great San Francisco Earthquake and Fire of 1906 killed about 700 people and wrecked about 250,000 homes.*

*Fire fighters at work in rescue operations (above)
and fighting an explosion (below).*

An 1835 fire in New York City (above) burned 650 buildings.

Glossary

Arson   The crime of starting a fire on purpose, with malice, and burning a building or other property

Backfire   A fire started on purpose to stop an advancing fire by creating a burned area in its path

Combustible   Capable of burning

Explosion   A violent fire that results from rapid expansion of gases

Fireboat   A boat equipped with fire-fighting gear, used to fight fires on ships or along a shoreline or waterfront

Fire drill   A practice exercise in fire safety procedures, especially practice in leaving a burning building safely

Firebreak   A strip of cleared land meant to stop the advance of a forest fire

Fire storm   A fire that creates its own strong wind currents

Fire truck   A truck equipped with fire-fighting gear

Flammable   Capable of being ignited easily and burning very rapidly

Fuel   A material that can be burned to produce heat or power

Oxygen   A colorless, tasteless, odorless gas that can create a fire when united rapidly with other substances; it is needed to keep a fire going

Smoke detector   An instrument that sounds an alarm when smoke begins to fill a room

Smoke inhalation   The breathing in of smoke instead of oxygen; the main cause of death or injury in a fire

Smoke jumper   A fire fighter who parachutes from an airplane to fight a forest fire

Spontaneous combustion   A fire that starts by itself when oxygen unites with certain other substances and creates a great amount of heat

Index· *Page numbers in boldface type indicate illustrations*

Photo Credits

FURNISHED BY THE SAN BERNARDINO CITY FIRE DEPARTMENT—Cover, pages 4, 7, 8, 10, 15, 16
COURTESY OF INA MUSEUM, PHILADELPHIA—Pages 2, 57, 58 (top and middle)
USDA/FOREST SERVICE—Pages 9, 22, 50 (top right), 59 (right)
JOHN WIECHERT—Pages 11, 13
HISTORICAL PICTURES SERVICE, INC., CHICAGO—Pages 19, 20, 29 (right), 30, 31, 38, 41, 46, 48, 56, 60, 62
STATE HISTORICAL SOCIETY OF WISCONSIN—Pages 23, 24
CHICAGO HISTORICAL SOCIETY—Pages 26 (left: ICHI-12924; right: ICHI-05734, Hesler-detail), 27, 28, 29 (left), 32, 33 (top: photo by Jex Bardwell; bottom: ICHI-02792)
COURTESY OF THE NEW YORK HISTORICAL SOCIETY, NEW YORK CITY—Page 36 (top photo by *Bronx Home News;* bottom photo by George Stonebridge, 1904)
COURTESY OF THE PUBLIC ARCHIVES OF NOVA SCOTIA—Pages 44, 45
DAVE BAUMHEFNER, NCAR—Page 50 (top left)
NOAA—Page 50 (bottom)
FIRE PREVENTION BUREAU, EVANSTON, ILLINOIS—Pages 53 (left), 58 (bottom)
THE GRAINGER BURN CENTER OF EVANSTON HOSPITAL—Pages 53 (right), 54
DAVID WAITE, LAS VEGAS SUN—Page 59 (left)
FRED TANNENBAUM, CHICAGO—Page 61

COVER PHOTO—Flames reached higher than forty feet during the 1980 Panorama Fire in San Bernardino, California.

About the Author

Dennis Fradin attended Northwestern University on a partial creative writing scholarship and graduated in 1967. He has published stories and articles in such places as *Ingenue, The Saturday Evening Post, Scholastic, Chicago, Oui,* and *National Humane Review.* His previous books include the Young People's Stories of Our States series for Childrens Press and *Bad Luck Tony* for Prentice-Hall. He is married and the father of three children.